The truth about wicca and witchcraft

James aten

First edition 2008

ISBN 978-0-6152-0945-6

This book is dedicated to my loving wife Kim.

Contents

Introduction

This is a book about Wicca as I have studied it. There is an ever-growing number of people interested in this subject and all Wiccan paths are not exactly the same. Indeed, the traditions of Wicca today are many and varying. Some feel a pull towards Celtic traditions, some may feel more compelled to study ancient Egyptian magick. Some may simply wish to study elements of several diferent paths to get the information that they need for their path. For beginners though, it's good to just stick with the basics. Once you've got them down, you can start to make educated decisions on what elements are going to be truly helpful to you.

When I began my studies, some 22 years ago, I knew intuitively that magick would work, but I was at a loss to explain exactly how. I knew that the more I learned about the subject, the more my confidence in my work would increase and the better my spells would work. So, in the early stages, I wanted to learn as much as I could about the process and everything that went into it. Needless to say, I ended up getting a lot more information than I expected! I was led down many avenues of knowledge and I wanted to share much of this information in my book.

You will find that on this path, you will experience many phases of learning and growth. The God and the Goddess will guide you whether you are aware of it or not. And when you meditate on a subject, prepare to get answers! My journey began when I did my first spell in 1986 and really kicked into high gear when I discovered the religion of Wicca in 1998. I was fortunate enough to have met a couple of teachers along the way who taught me exactly what I needed to know, when I needed to know it. The rest, I got from great books.

My hope is that after you read this book, you will have a very clear understanding of how Wicca works, how Witchcraft works, and why. Much of the information I have included here is put in place as a guideline to help you develop insight for yourself and bring about positive

changes. It's also to help you avoid the same painful mistakes that some of us have made.

It's always been my belief that knowledge is power and you should get your information from

more than one source, so I have included relevant information about Wicca, the Occult,

and general Metaphysics. At the end of the book there is a recommended reading section.

Some of you may choose to enjoy these books as I have. Blessed Be

Chapter 1

What Wicca is All About

Welcome to the world of Wicca. There has been much said about our religion, and much of it is misinformation. The goal of this book is to educate you, the reader, on what Wicca is really all about and dispel the myths. So, I think we should begin by dumping the garbage and false information about Wicca.. First of all, Wicca is NOT about Demonology, Satan or Devil worship, the Necronomicon, or "Black Magick". These things have absolutely nothing to do with Wicca.. They are not associated in any way shape or form. The Devil is a Christian concept and is not worshiped, hated, loved, or even acknowledged in Wicca.. I run a Wiccan chat group on the internet and I constantly get requests to join from people claiming to be vampires, Satan worshippers, and even werewolves. What any of that has to do with Wicca is beyond me. I have to just assume these people must be sadly misinformed if they think any of this makes them Wiccan. True, the one that claimed to be a Lycan made us laugh, but I always have to advise these people to do some research on what Wicca really is before they run around saying they're Wiccan. If your goal is to conjure a Demon, or learn how to make a Voodoo doll to get revenge on someone, you will not find what you are looking for here. These things fall under the category of "Wrong thinking". If you are tempted to do something of that nature, there is a better way to handle your problem. The fact is, you DO have power and you CAN fix your problems! But doing something with harmful intent, or lashing out at people will only defeat your purpose and bring more negativity raining down on you. Also, it's important to note here that the law of karma is universal. Just because someone doesn't believe in it doesn't mean that it won't affect them. I have met young people who have said to me, "I don't have to follow the law of three, because I'm not Wiccan". This is entirely inaccurate. It's never okay to harm someone else, and you will never really just "get away with it".

Another thing that's noteworthy here is that the things you see in movies and on T.V

Are almost completely fantasy. There is very little, if any, reality in movies like "The Craft" or T.V shows like "Charmed". I have met people, also, who actually think the things they see on the screen are real! There is nothing much to be learned from movies or T.V for the beginner. In the ensuing chapters, I will be covering the complete concept of Wicca.. I will also explain some of the differences, and surprising similarities, to other religions. And I will be covering subjects that are closely related to Wicca, such as meditation, psychic development, chakras, auras, astral travel, and, of course, Witchcraft! My goal is for you to have a complete understanding of what Wicca is about. After reading this book, all the myths, and things you might have heard about Wicca in Church, should be dispelled completely. There is no evil to be found here, just people on a very old Spiritual path reaching for the Divine.

Wicca is a religion, and our belief system actually predates Christianity by thousands of years. Wiccans do not see God as an entirely male Deity, nor do we see God as some far away distant force. We see the Divine in all things. In all of nature we can see that there is a male and female aspect at work, so it makes sense that the Divine would be represented that way as well. All things are of the same source, so how can we say the Divine is only male or female, when it is both, and, more importantly, it is ALL. As Wiccans we are taught to have reverence for all life. That means animals, plants, and, of course, trees. All living things must be respected, as well as the planet itself. Having empathy is a good trait. Most people don't have trouble realizing that animals feel pain and fear, as well as happiness and sadness. But there are some who do. Harder, perhaps, to grasp is the fact that plant life is also life, and even possesses a very simplistic form of consciousness. We don't see ourselves as dominators of the Earth, but rather as caretakers. Pollution and the oncoming threat of global warming should be major concerns. After all, since we all live here, doesn't it make sense to take care of the place we live? So the Wiccan Rede which states "Do as you will, and harm none" applies not only to people. And that includes not doing anything to harm yourself as well. The full version of the Rede will be covered in a later chapter. It's a set of guidelines for Witchcraft, being in tune with nature, developing your true inner power and wisdom, and learning how to work for the good of all.

There are some who claim Wicca is not ancient, and it's a fairly recent invention. This is not exactly the case. Wicca is basically a modern revival of ancient Pagan beliefs. Belief systems that existed long before the invention of modern Christianity. It's believed by many, in fact, that the original teachings of Jesus actually referred to such things as karma and reincarnation. Most commonly, Wiccan beliefs are linked to Shamanic, Celtic, and ancient Egyptian beliefs, as well as Hinduism and Buddhism. And, yes, in Wicca, it's perfectly acceptable to do Witchcraft! It is important to note here, however, that not all Wiccans practice Witchcraft, and not all Witches are Wiccan. Being Wiccan means you live by the Wiccan Rede, honor the God and Goddess,and celebrate the Wiccan holidays (known as Sabbats). You can do this with or without doing the actual practice of Witchcraft.

Witchcraft is actually quite safe if you go about it the right way. There are procedures and steps you must take to insure that your spell comes out right, and doesn't cause any inadvertent harm. This cannot be taken lightly! "Do as you will and harm none" is a lot like the Wiccan version of the ten commandments, and we go by that for a reason. I will be covering the reasons for that in depth in later chapters.

The true goal in Wicca should be to get in touch with your higher spiritual self. When your higher self is in control, you are aligned with your true purpose here. When your lower self is in control, you are obsessed by Earthly matters that spiritually are of no real importance. For example, there's one individual I know who is obsessed with looking important and trying to impress or intimidate others. This person claims to be a teacher, but he's really a slave to his lower self, and will have many hard karmic lessons to learn before he can advance to a higher spiritual level. And, after all, that is EVERYONE'S ultimate goal.

The Pentacle

The most sacred symbol of our religion is the Pentacle. This is another thing that people have a tendency to misinterpret, thinking it to be a symbol of "the Devil". The inverted pentagram was adopted as a symbol of Satanism, but even it has other meanings. The Pentacle in Wicca is a pentagram with one point up, two points down, and a circle around it. It has had many different meanings in a lot of different belief systems through the ages.

Of course, we're going to focus on what this symbol means in Wicca. To Wiccans this symbol represents the ELEMENTS. Earth, Air, Fire, Water and Spirit (also known as Akasha). This symbol can be seen on most Wiccan altars, and is used very often in magick. It's also worn as a pendant to protect against harm. Here is an illustration of the Pentacle and what it represents.

At the top point of the pentacle (or Pentagram, also used in Wicca) is SPIRIT. Spirit represents your higher spiritual self, and your higher goals. That's the reason it's on top, because the spiritual is always more important than the material. When you do magick, your spell always begins on the astral or thought plane before it manifests on the physical plane. Here are the magickal purposes associated with these elements:

Air - Thought and communication

Fire - Fiery emotions, passion, courage, change

Water - Intuition, psychic abilities, emotion
Earth - Abundance, nurturing, growth

Colors associated with the elements:

Akasha - White or purple

Air - Yellow

Water - Blue

Fire - Red

Earth - Green

This also goes for the Pentagram, which is the star alone without the circle. The circle around the Pentacle represents life, spiritual growth, and rebirth.

Chapter 2

The Wiccan Rede

This is the set of rules every Wiccan lives by. Don't worry if you can't memorize the whole thing right away. Remember that everything takes time to master. You're probably not going to become a perfect Wiccan overnight. It's a long path, and we all continue learning for many years. Once you begin the Wiccan path, however, you will begin to see positive changes in your life almost right away. You will begin a journey of learning more about the world, and yourself. It will transform you into a wiser person. So, without further ado, here it is. The poem we know as "The Rede of the Wiccae" or The Wiccan Rede.

1. Bide the Wiccan laws ye must, in perfect love and perfect trust.

2. Live and let live, fairly take and fairly give.

3. Cast the circle thrice about to keep all evil spirits out.

4. To bind the spell every time, let the spell be spake in rhyme.

5. Soft of eye, light of touch - speak little, listen much.

6. Doesil go by the waxing moon - sing and dance the Wiccan rune.

7. Widdershins go when the moon doth wane, and the werewolf howls by the dread wolfsbane

8. When the Lady's moon is new, kiss the hand to her times two.

9. When the moon rides at her peak, then your heart's desire seek.

10. Heed the Northwind's mighty gale - lock the door and drop the sail.

11. When the wind comes from the South, love will kiss thee on the mouth.

12. When the wind blows from the East, expect the new and set the feast.

13. When the West wind blows o'er thee, departed spirits restless be.

14. Nine woods in the cauldron go - burn them quick and burn them slow.

15. Elder be ye Lady's tree - burn it not, or cursed ye'll be.

16. When the wheel begins to turn, let the Beltane fires burn.

17. When the wheel has turned a Yule, light the log and let Pan rule.

18. Heed ye flower, bush, and tree - by the Lady blessed be.

19. Where the rippling waters go, cast a stone an truth ye'll know.

20. When ye have need, harken not to others greed.

21. With the foll no season spend, or be counted as his friend.

22. Merry meet and merry part, bright the cheeks an warm the heart.

23. Mind the threefold law ye should - three times bad an three times good.

24. When misfortune is enow, wear the blue star on thy brow.

25. True in love ever be, unless thy lover's false to thee.

26. Eight words the Wiccan Rede fulfill - an it harm none, do what you will.

   I realize some of you newcomers may be sitting there scratching your heads right about now, but not to worry. I'm going to provide the full explanation here, line by line, of exactly what this poem means. The basic rules that Wiccans follow I think are pretty self explanatory, but there are other elements included in the Rede that include magick, and celebration of Wiccan holidays.

1. Trust in the laws that the Lord and Lady have set. They are loving Deities, and following these laws is to your benefit.

2. Basically, don't ever be a bigot, or fill your heart with hate. Understand that everyone is in the same boat here, no matter what differences they have.

3. Before doing a spell, a Witch generally will cast a circle. This does serve the purpose of

keeping bad energies out while you are working, among other things.

4. Speaking the spell in rhyme keeps the conscious mind occupied while the subconscious mind puts the magick to work.

5. Never brag, be a loudmouth, or pretend to know things that you really don't. The way to gain wisdom is by listening.

6. When the Moon is waxing (getting bigger), this is the time to draw things to you. You can do this by going around the circle clockwise.

7. When the Moon is waning (getting smaller), this is the time to banish negative energy. You do this by going around the circle counter-clockwise.

8. On the night of the new Moon (return of the Goddess) we salute her by kissing two fingers.

9. On the night of the full moon, do a spell to bring your heart's desire to you.

10. The North wind can be very powerful. And cold!

11. The South wind is warm, and South is the direction of passion.

12. East is the direction of new beginnings. The Sun ries in the East.

13. West is the direction you face when doing necromancy.

14. In rituals to celebrate the Sabbats, there traditionally are 9 woods that are burned : Apple, Birch, Fir, Hawthorne, Hazel, Oak, Rowan, Vine and Willow.

15. Elder is the tree that is never to be burned in ritual because it's sacred to the Lady.

16. The wheel of the year is made up of all the lesser and greater Sabbats. Beltane is one of those Sabbats.

17. Yule is the Winter Sabbat.

18. Have respect for all things in nature. To do so is to honor the Goddess.

19. Remember how your actions affect things and people around you. It's like ripples in a pond, so try to create positive change.

20. Never accept money for the use of the power.

21. If you spend time with a fool, other people may begin to think you're a fool as well.

22. Spending time with friends and exchanging positive energy is a good thing.

23. Always remember that the energy you put out there comes back to you.

24. This is actually an old occult trick that protects you from psychic attack. It protects you from other things as well.

25. Be faithful to the one you love. If they don't return the favor, then don't waste your time.

26. These eight words sum it all up !

Blessed be

Chapter 3

The Importance of Karma

Karma is the universal law that applies to each and every one of us. It means simply that everything you do will come back to you. In Wiccan terms it's known as the threefold law. Whether it can actually be measured as three time is debatable, of course. Sometimes it can feel like three times, or even ten times. It not only applies to magick, but your every day life as well. It is through karma that we learn our life lessons. Not only in this lifetime, but in successive lifetimes. The goal is to become the best person you can in this lifetime. The ultimate goal is to eliminate wrong thinking entirely. So what is wrong thinking? Prejudice, hatred, self-righteousness, violent, destructive or self destructive attitudes, these are all examples of wrong thinking.

To clarify the point here, there is a belief that , in Wiccan terms, is known as the Spiral. The Spiral represents the development of a soul who progresses through various lifetimes slowly, or perhaps very quickly, moving up the Spiral. Beginning with the most base earthly needs, the person first masters the physical world. There are, of course, many mistakes along the way. This is where karma comes into play. The purpose of this cause and effect action is to teach us not to repeat these same mistakes. As we progress up the Spiral, we learn such certain traits such as love, unity, being non-judgmental, and shedding selfishness, hate, and bigotry. We then begin to reap the full rewards of spirituality. Psychic awareness is open, and Divine inspiration is free to enter the body and guide us. At the top of the Spiral, we may choose to give up physical life completely, and rejoin with the All.

What's important to remember is that we are all on different paths that eventually will lead to the same place. We simply are all at different stages in our development. We all get there eventually, so the thought that one is better than someone else is actually inaccurate. You have to work to nurture the correct attitude if you're going to advance spiritually. Karma is a natural teaching tool, but knowledge, and the ability to apply that knowledge, is a great help. This is also the reason we have guidelines in Wicca like the "harm none" rule. If you understand it and follow it correctly, you can actually avoid some of the more painful lessons that karma teaches. In order to not cause harm with a spell, sometimes you have to think. Think about the spell and all it's possible outcomes. You don't want to do a money spell that will result in you being seriously injured and suing somebody. When in doubt, just include the line "with harm to none" in your spell.

The techniques in Wicca are completely safe as long as you know what you're doing. Some tools such as the Ouija board are not recommended. They can open doorways to the lower astral plane, which some of us like to refer to as "the psych ward". The spirits that dwell there are not always friendly and not always very helpful either. They can give wrong information and even prank you. They can even be very angry and refuse to leave once the board is put away. Not something you want to have to deal with, as some of the more irate ones can be difficult to get rid of. Similar to the way that some obnoxious people can be hard to get rid of sometimes.

Remember that harming none includes harming yourself ! So, now that we've gone over bad karma, did I mention there's also good karma? Good karma comes from truly good actions. It doesn't work so well when you do good things, but for completely selfish reasons. And it absolutely does not work when you do things only for the purpose of getting a karmic reward. What you put out there is what you are going to get back. And if you do nothing but negative things in this lifetime, it will follow you to your next one.

Now, there are people that will tell you that evil has it's place in the grand scheme of things. It's part of the balance and must be accepted. This view is not inaccurate. All the events happening on this plane are part of the Divine order in some way, and even bad events often serve as teaching tools for us. All you have to do sometimes is ask yourself "what did I learn from this?" However, what we're talking about here is moving UP the Spiral. Mastering yourself, you slowly rise above the earthly muck, and finally begin to see things clearly. People do move up the Spiral continuously. Sometimes whether they are aware of it or not. But being aware of it, would you really want to go on experiencing the constraints of earthly karma? Or open up your awareness and rise above it? Every Wiccan is responsible for their own decisions and their own actions. The choice is always yours.

It's true that Wicca is considered a Pagan religion. Some people may be quick to point out that in ancient times Pagans committed acts such as human sacrifice. Throughout history great civilizations have risen and fallen. The same with belief systems. Societies that once possessed great knowledge have suffered over time from invasions, disasters and human greed. Records were destroyed, lost or discarded over time, and belief systems degenerated. Temples that were once places of worship were then used for sacrifice, because it had been long forgotten what they were built for. This can be said not only for Pagans, but for Christians as well. When they began to kill those who didn't believe as they did, they themselves became guilty of human sacrifice. The teachings of their own Jesus had been altered to justify such acts. Remember that anytime someone points a finger, there are three pointing back.

And what about the destruction of our own planet? When you're in tune with nature and your own psychic senses, you can feel the energy imbalance of the world. It's as if Mother Earth herself is weeping in pain. This may be the ultimate example of karma. For so many years people have been taking and taking from the Earth. Apparently believing that they were put here to be dominant. Putting themselves above everything except their God. Polluting the Earth and atmosphere. This blatant and sometimes ignorant disregard has led to the decline of

19

conditions here. So what we learn from this is that continuing on a destructive path eventually leads to your own destruction.

Even in modern day quantum physics, the law of cause and effect is still recognized. And karma is also the belief in many other religions worldwide, and has been for thousands of years. In ancient Egypt, the Goddess Ma'at represented karmic justice. She was the weigher of souls. In Egyptian mythology, Ma'at held a scale. On the left was the heart, which represented the soul, and on the right was a feather. If the soul was heavier than the feather, that meant the heart was heavy, and there was karmic sludge in the soul. It was judged by the God Osiris whether the soul would pass on to be free from Earthly karma or have to go back for more tests. The symbol of Ma'ats scale is still used by Witches today in situations in which justice is called for.

To simplify, think about all the times in your life when you've done something wrong and KNEW it was wrong. You had the feeling something bad would happen because of it, and sure enough something did, so you learned your lesson. That's karma at work.

Chapter 4

Meditation and Visualization

Meditation and visualization are very important for awakening your psychic abilities. Meditation is a simple matter, but must be performed on a regular basis to be effective. The preferred method is to practice at the same time every night after sundown. The more diligently you work at it, the more effective it will be for you. It is usually recommended that you begin your meditation sitting in an upright position, with your hands resting on your legs palms up. However, if you have trouble getting completely comfortable in that position, you may just try lying on your back with your hands on your stomach. The first thing you will need to do is make sure there will be no outside distractions. Make sure the T.V. is off, the phone is of, etc. Then you will need to make sure that you are completely relaxed. You may try flexing and relaxing every muscle in your body, from your toes, to the top of your head, until there is absolutely no tension, and your body has reached a point of total relaxation.

The next step is to slow down your breathing. By slowing down your breathing, you are actually slowing down your brain activity. Sometimes stray thoughts will start to pop into your head while you are doing this, gently push them out and focus on your breathing. You may start by counting to three as you inhale, holding the breath for a count of three, then counting to three as you exhale. Then slow your breathing down as slow as you can get it, taking slow deep breaths. You can dim the lights and put on soft music to help you relax if you wish, or burn incense. The goal is to achieve a state of blackness and non thought. The first couple of times you do it, you may fall asleep. If you fall asleep, that's okay! You probably needed the sleep. Soon, however, you will train yourself not to fall asleep, and you will reach your goal.

Once you have mastered this technique, you may want to begin some visualization exercises. Visualization is a very important part of Witchcraft. One very good one is to simply visualize the colors of the spectrum. This will help you to open up your third eye and increase your psychic awareness. Visualize them in this order, Red, Orange, Yellow, Green, Blue, Indigo, Violet. There are many other exercises, and I will list a few of them here. Later on, you may even want to make up your own. For each one, you will want to sit down, close your eyes, and go into a light meditative state. You will want to see nothing but a black screen to begin with.

Exercise 1. The Spiral

Visualize a line of blue light. Starting at the bottom of your sight and going upwards and around into a widening spiral. Hold the image for a moment, then visualize it receding downwards, back into nothing. Repeat this a few times.

Exercise 2. Color Balls

Visualize a red ball in the right corner of your vision. Now see it moving in an up and down zigzag pattern and going left until it disappears from view. Noe do the same with a ball from each color of the spectrum. These are also the colors of your CHAKRAS, which we will be talking more about later.

Exercise 3. The Chalkboard

There is an exercise where you visualize a chalkboard in front of you. On the chalkboard, you can write or draw anything you wish, you then will erase it when you're done. Each time you erase, tell yourself " I can visualize whatever I want, whenever I want." This one is especially helpful for people who have a hard time visualizing.

The color exercises are developed specifically to help you open your third eye chakra. The others are for general visualization. You need the ability to visualize in order to do spells, and for other tasks such as astral projection. The repeating of statements such as the one above while in this state serve to program your subconscious mind in a positive way. Your subconscious mind basically does what it's told to do, so if you tell it you CAN do something, then you will believe that you can do it. For the most part, if you believe you can do something, then you will be able to do it. That's not to say that you'll be able to fly, but it is a confidence booster. Confidence helps you in everyday life and in magick.

Higher Self

Now, the best source I've found for information is your higher self. Your higher self is YOU. It's the part of you that exists high on the spiritual plane. It's also your connection to the Divine. The Divine Source is also known as The All, and the God and Goddess are said to be the male and female principles of this source. So, once you've mastered the meditation and you've opened your psychic awareness, you may want to actually ask questions of your higher self. In the astral plane, there is no such thing as time or space, so you have access to infinite knowledge. You can also make requests of your higher self while in a psychic state and have them answered. Ask your higher self to help you make your goals manifest, and you will be surprised at the help you receive. Some people might suggest you try to contact spirits, or what have you, but I'm of a mind that going directly to the source is best. Frequent contact with your higher self is beneficial to you in the sense that what you get is always good, and in your best interest spiritually as well. Also, spirits, aside from your guide of course, may have their own agenda. Some dwell on the lower astral plane, and have no real interest in being helpful to anyone. Your higher self will never steer you wrong.

Buddhist Meditation

Some meditation techniques used by Wiccans, I've found, are very similar to Buddhist techniques. These are designed, as in Buddhism, to help you shed your own bad karma and negative behaviors and, ultimately, to achieve enlightenment. It has long been my belief that our own spirit guides are those who have already mastered their karmic lessons. In Buddhism, this would be comparable to one who has achieved enlightenment, or a Buddha. One method that I use is the daily review. Each night, before you go to bed, mentally review your day. Think about the things that you did well, and think about the things you didn't handle so well. Did you start an argument or treat somebody harshly that you probably shouldn't have? Handle a situation poorly? Do you feel guilty about something you did? Don't beat yourself up. Sit and reflect on the situation for a moment. Think about the reason WHY you behaved that way. Now think about ways you could have handled it better. If you still don't come up with an answer, try meditating on it.

You also can meditate on teachings from a trusted teacher. This can help you to deepen your understanding of what you've learned. When you sit quietly and focus on only your breathing, it calms your mind. It's usually full of chatter and clutter. Calming the mind this way helps you to be more calmer, more relaxed, and less stressed in everyday life. For improving your concentration, visualize an image of the Buddha and meditate on it for a while. There is also a Buddhist purification. For this, you simply visualize Buddha, and then visualize light radiating from the Buddha and into yourself. I bet you'll be surprised at how good you feel afterwards! I believe that all these techniques are beneficial whether you are Buddhist, Wiccan, a practicing psychic, or simply meditating for relaxation. And, really, who COULDN'T use a little relaxation? Remember, when you're calm and everything is quiet is when your psychic mind speaks to you.

Chapter 5

Psychic Protection

Psychic protection is important when you feel people are projecting negative energy your way, or in the event of an actual psychic attack! Anyone who is thinking angry or hateful thoughts about you is sending some negative energy your way. While this is not an actual attack, the negative energy can have a bad effect on your aura. An actual psychic attack is a concentrated effort on the part of a practitioner involving negative thoughts and magick. While this is not likely to happen very often, it's always good to be prepared. And a little aura cleansing every so often is good for you regardless. Anybody can have a buildup of auric sludge or psychic ick after prolonged exposure to negative energy, whether it's somebody else's, or even your own. Here, I will list some of my favorite and most effective techniques for psychic self defense, and some for preventative maintenance.

The Tower of Light

Stand up straight with your arms at your sides. Relax your body and breathe steadily. Visualize your aura as a blue oval shape surrounding you. Then visualize a globe of pure white light just a couple feet over your head. Relax for a moment and when you're ready, say mentally, or out loud, "I aspire to the greatest good that I can achieve". Then see the light come flowing down, filling your aura, and you, with a brilliant white light. You should see it as light with silver sparkles in it. Keep in mind that the light will continue flowing even after your visualization stops .It's recommended that you do this exercise two to three times daily. Done on a regular basis, this can strengthen your aura, and possibly even aid your spiritual development. The white globe represents your higher self. The light is Divine light, and is of a very high spiritual vibration. When it fills your aura, it will actually raise the vibrations of your aura, which is what makes it stronger. This, in turn, will increase your aura's ability to protect you from harm.

The Pentagram

Another method is the pentagram on the forehead. This is for when you are actually under a psychic attack. When your psychic awareness has been sufficiently developed, you most likely will become aware of a psychic attack if it happens. As I said, this is very unlikely to happen, mainly due to the fact that there are very few people who are able, or willing for that matter, to actually perform one. However, I believe you should always be prepared. You may occasionally run across Dark Magick practitioners, and I believe there's never any reason at all to be intimidated by them. Karma is on your side, not theirs, and a Witch has a strong will. You must never allow yourself to be intimidated. So, if you suspect you may be under an attack, calmly walk around the room in a circle clockwise. If someone is attacking you, you will feel an odd tingling. Probably in your third eye, although there was a time that I did it, and I felt it in my third eye and tingling down through my chest. The point where you feel that indicates the direction the attack is coming from. Turn and face the attack and step forward Now, raise your hands to your forehead and with your thumbs and forefingers, make the shape of a triangle. Visualize a pentagram of blue light on your forehead, or any other symbol that you strongly associate with protection. Forcefully fling the symbol at your attacker. This will stop the attack immediately. Then perform the above tower of light. On the following page is an image of what the procedure would look like.

34

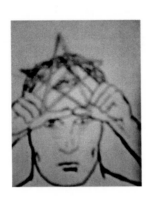

Mirrors

Another method is to visualize yourself surrounded by mirrors. If you are under a psychic

or magickal attack, the mirrors will simply deflect the negative energy back on the attackers.

Mirrors are also used in spells to reflect back negative energy that's sent out to you.

Incenses

Listed below are some incenses that have high spiritual vibrations. These can be used to

cleanse a room of negative energy. Listed will be some of the most commonly used and easy to

find.

Anise seed

Ash

Basil

Bay

Birch

Blackberry

Cinnamon

Coriander

Dragon's Blood

Elder

Frankincense

Garlic

Ginger

Ginseng
Hawthorn

Juniper

Lavender

Mugwort

Myrrh

Nightshade

Oak

Pine

Rose

Rosemary

Sage

Sandalwood

St. John's Wort

Star Anise

Sunflower

Thyme

Tobacco

Chapter 6

Witchcraft

You DO have personal power and you CAN make things happen. Even in quantum physics it's been noted that we can affect things around us just by observing them. All it takes for Witchcraft is a little preparation, energy, will power and concentration.

Preparation

To prepare for a spell, you will need the proper supplies and tools. These can be store bought or handmade. Generally, there will be candles, incense, and herbs involved, as well as symbols, runes, and sometimes stones that correlate with your magickal intent. There are other special tools in traditional Witchcraft, such as the Athame, Bolline, chalice, and yes, a wand. There are many combinations, and many different ways to do a spell, and I will give some examples here. In the end, however, the best way to do it is whatever way feels right to you. Above all else, it's important that you feel comfortable doing the spell, and CONFIDENT that it will work.

Tools

1. Athame - The Athame is a double edged, black handled knife that is used for cutting energy.
2. Bolline - The Bolline is a white handled knife with a curved blade that is used it's used for cutting things like herbs, candles, etc. in preparation for ritual. It also represents the male aspect.
3. Chalice - This is used to drink wine from during ritual. It also may be used to make an offering to a particular God or Goddess.
4. Wand - The Wand is a special tool used for directing energy.
5. Candles - These are generally dressed with oil and charged with your personal energy.

Keep in mind though, the purpose of your magickal tools is mostly to keep your mind focused on your magickal goal. Certain colors and symbols actually speak to your subconscious mind, letting it know that it's time to do magick, and further, helping you to focus on your intent

.

In the early stages, these tools are most important. Later, things will come a little easier for you, and you won't rely so much on them. You may shed the wand at times and just focus your energy through your finger for example. However, you will always have items that you love, and would never get rid of, as I do myself. Always remember; the energy comes from YOU.

Casting a Circle

Before beginning any spell, it's wise to create a circle. A circle is your protective space. It serves the dual purpose of containing your energy until it's ready to be released and keeping out any stray astral entities who may be attracted to the energy. Your visualization skills will be utilized here, as you will need to visualize your energy as a white light. You'll see it flowing out of you through the tip of your wand (and if you don't yet have a wand, you can make one with a tree branch and maybe a quartz crystal tip. Be creative!) and down to the ground. You will need to go around clockwise in a circle. Once you have completed a circle of energy, see the energy rising up, making walls around you, and finally enclosing as a dome over your head. You'll definitely want to make sure you have everything you need for the spell with you first, so you don't have to go outside to get anything.

Raising Energy

Once the circle is cast, you will need to raise energy for your spell. This is your personal energy, and it can be raised a variety of ways, including: dancing, drumming, flexing muscles, or a variety of physical activities you can perform inside the circle. Your energy will take the form of a cone. Personally, I enjoy playing loud music and drumming along. The music

helps me to build up more energy. The circle becomes the base of your cone. Once you feel you have built up enough energy, release it into whatever magickal tool you're using. For me it's usually a candle. Grab the candle and channel all of that energy into it. While you do this, visualize your magick happening. Remember not to let your thoughts stray during this process. For the spell to work properly, you have to maintain focus on your goal, and be confident that your spell will work. After you have charged the candle with your energy and intent, light it to send the energy out. Once it has been sent out, your spell is complete. You can now break your circle and step out.

Oils

Another part of Witchcraft is the use of essential oils. There are many different uses for these, including aromatherapy, but the main concern here will be how to use them in spellwork. The main thing that I use them for is dressing candles. Basically, this means rubbing oil on your candle as part of your preparation. If you want to draw something to you, start at the ends of the candle and work your way towards the middle. If you're sending energy out, start at the middle and go out towards the ends. There are all kinds of oils to suit your magickal needs, and I will list some here to get you started.

Enhance psychic abilities - Acacia, Anise, Lemongrass, Lilac, Mimosa, Nutmeg, Sandalwood.

Enhance power - Carnation, Rosemary, Vanilla.

Enhance luck - Cinnamon, Cypress, Lotus.

Bring happiness - Apple blossom, Sweetpea, Tuberose

Bring peace - Benzoin, Cumin, Gardenia, Magnolia, Tuberose.

Healing - Carnation, Eucalyptus, Gardenia, Lotus, Myrrh, Narcissus, Rosemary, Sandalwood, Violet.
For harmony - Basil, Gardenia, Lilac, Narcissus.

Bring money - Almond, Bayberry, Bergamot, Honeysuckle, Mint, Patchouli, Pine, Vervain.

Lust - Cinnamon, Clove, Musk, Vanilla.

Break hexes - Bergamot, Myrrh, Rose Geranium, Rosemary, Rue, Vetivert.

Purification - Acacia, Cinnamon, Clove, Frankincense, Jasmine, Lavender, Myrrh,

Olive, Sandalwood.

Protection - Cypress, Myrrh, Patchouli, Rose Geranium, Rosemary, Rue, Violet.

Meditation - Acacia, Hyacinth, Jasmine, Magnolia, Myrrh, Nutmeg.

Love - Clove, Gardenia, Jasmine, Orris, Rose.

Why Witchcraft Works

At this point, you may be wondering how Witchcraft works. The reason why it works is because you are much more than just your physical self. You are connected with the Divine! Whether you know it or not. There is a whole other world out there beyond the physical world. It's invisible to the human eye, and can only be through your third eye. It's an extra "eye" that lies between your eyebrows. The pituitary gland and pineal gland in your brain are said to be remnants of this third eye, and it's believed that our earliest ancestors had a fully developed version. You also have bodies in the etheric, and astral bodies, which will be covered fully in this book as well. You will need to stop thinking solely about the physical world and be aware of these planes. As above, so below is a phrase you will become well acquainted with. The after reading all this book, you should begin to understand how this all works. But the best, and most fun way to know is to see it happening for yourself.

Sample Spells

Here I decided to include 2 sample spells. You can use these as they are, or add your own touches to them. With practice and experience, you may want to create some of your own.

If your first spell doesn't work, do it again and keep doing it until it does. It may take some time to get the technique down, but when you begin to see the results of your first spell, there's nothing like it. Remember to cast your circle and have all items needed inside before you proceed.

Spell to bring love

Remember when doing a love spell not to name any specific person, because that would be impinging on the persons free will and that would only backfire on you. If you do a spell for money, make sure that the outcome won't cause harm to anyone. You wouldn't want insurance money from your house burning down or a terrible accident. When in doubt, add the words "With harm to none" in your spell. Think carefully about the attributes you want in your mate, and what you want and need out of the relationship. Make a list if you have to. You will need the following items : 1 red candle, Patchouli oil, Patchouli or Rose incense. Carve a heart or a love rune on the candle. Dress the candle, light the incense, and perform the spell as described previously. Use an incantation such as "Goddess bring love to me, from loneliness I will be free" or make up your own if you like. When you finish, set the candle in a window where it can get moonlight. The night of the full moon is always best, as the moon and the Goddess, are at their peak.

Protection Spell

For this spell you will need : 1 white candle, Dragon's Blood oil, Dragon's Blood or Frankincense and Myrrh incense. This spell will be performed in the same manner, except you may want to evoke a protective Deity. Choose whichever one feels right to you. For a list of Deities, see the chapter "Gods and Goddesses". You also may want to visualize a white light or a net of white light around you while doing this spell. This light will stay with you for several weeks after. Then if you feel the need, do another one.

Candle Colors

Many Witches are very particular about candle color. Certain colors have a certain energy which can be helpful to your spell. Your intent matters more than anything else and

sometimes if a color feels right to you, then you should just go with it. Having said that, here's a list of candle colors and what they're most commonly used for.

Red- Energy, strength, emotional stimulation, generate power, sexual stimulation, love.

Orange- Stimulating color, helps to attract people and get results.

Yellow- Attraction, persuasion, study, divination.

Green- Growth, health, finances, good luck, fertility, employment.

Blue- Serenity, peace, tranquility, creative expression, patience, healing.

Dark Blue- Psychic awareness, wisdom, cause change.

Purple- Power, ambition, spiritual development, connecting with cosmic consciousness, healing serious illness.

Pink- Love, release depression, increase friendship.

White- positive energy, good will, meditation, magick, purification, reflect negative energy.

Brown- Earth candle, stability, security, animal healing.

Black- Absorb and banish negative energy, banishing.

Self Dedication

In Wicca it's traditional to do a self dedication rite. For those who are new to Wicca, I will cover what this involves. Though there are many different types of self dedication rites and honestly, you can do whichever one you're most comfortable with, or even write your own, I think there's a few basic things you should think about. You will be approaching the Lord and Lady for the rite, so it's best to do so with openness and honesty. It's important in Witchcraft to be honest with yourself above all else. It's also important to know your craft, and understand the way spells work and what their affects can be. At some point, you will also be choosing a magickal name. This is a name that you use in ritual. Basically, it should be a name that makes a statement about what you represent and what you aspire to be.

Now, for the rite itself, you will first want to do a ritual bath. This would be a regular bath, basically, with some salt thrown into the water to cleanse negative energy. Then you can meditate or sit in contemplation on your path, and what you may wish to learn about and achieve. Then cast your circle and evoke the Lord and Lady in perfect love and perfect trust. They will already know who you are, but you may introduce yourself anyway. Let them know that you are truly dedicating yourself to this path, and vow to do your very best to use the power only for good with harm to no one. Know that if there are any mistakes along the way, they will help to guide you so you can learn from them. I am including an incantation here as an example. Feel free to use this one if you like.

Lord and Lady, hear my words this night

Embrace me in your Divine light

Open is the way, open is the door
Open to me forevermore.
Bring me enlightenment, show me the way

Protect me by night and by day.

Chapter 7

Gods and Goddesses

In Wicca we recognize the male and female aspect of the Divine. The manifestation of the Divine here on Earth, we refer to as the God and Goddess or Lord and Lady. We do not see the Divine as some far away distant force watching us from above, but rather we see the Divine in all things. Including ourselves. This view is anything but new. It was even found in the Egyptian "Book of the Dead". Specifically in a passage where the recently deceased Ani proclaims " My soul is God, my soul is eternity."

Of course there are also many pantheons of Gods and Goddesses. From Egyptian to Celtic to Norse. The various Gods and Goddesses can be seen simply as aspects or different "faces" of the Lord and Lady. Faces of the Divine. In Wicca, we may choose to evoke these Deities and ask them to assist with our magick. To do this, you first have to choose the right Deity for your magickal purpose. For example : Venus for a spell to bring love, Thor for protection. You raise the energy and send it to the Deity, who will safely direct it towards your goal. This could be considered the Wiccan version of a prayer !

So, you can see by now why the idea that this is nothing but "idol worship" or that this practice will lead you to "the Devil" is pretty silly. Those ideas were created by people who wanted to take away your personal power so that a few people could be in control of everyone. The character of the Devil was created for a dual purpose. First: to scare people into converting (Which wasn't hard after books were burned and laws were created to keep people from reading) and second: in an attempt to make Pagan religions look evil. His appearance was patterned after Pagan horned Gods, such as Pan, in an attempt to do just that. When you discover Wicca, that means the time has come for you to re-discover your power. I consider that a very positive thing! It's a gift that only needs to be nurtured and applied with wisdom.

It may confuse people as to why so many religions have so many different versions of what God is. What I've discovered is that the Divine is the same everywhere. Only the names, stories and imagery change. These changes are usually based on local culture, or the ideas of the people at the time the particular religion was created. The important thing is what you get out of it. Some people use information to advance themselves spiritually, and some use it to justify their own negativity. Some people may tell you that their religion is the only way, and I believe that is a very narrow minded view. You aren't going to hear me say that about Wicca either. I would never seek to disregard the great spiritual teachings of Buddhism, or Hinduism, or even the teachings of Jesus. I believe that if you look close enough, you will see the wisdom there as well. The truth is that we all are on different paths, and they all will lead us back to the Divine Source at some point. But I WILL say that Wicca is the right choice for a growing number of people. That includes myself, obviously. So, with that explanation out of the way, I will now present these examples of Gods and Goddesses from pantheons all around the world. I am also including a brief description of what each one represents, this will give you an idea of which ones to evoke, or invoke, when you're doing magick. You can choose any one you like, and you may even feel drawn to a particular pantheon. Again, I will list the ones who are most commonly invoked.

Egyptian

Isis - The original mother Goddess. She's also associated with fertility, magick, and resurrection.

Osiris- Husband of Isis, and God of fertility and resurrection. Also judges a souls cleanliness upon death.

Horus - Son of Isis and Osiris. Known as the solar avenger who avenged his father's death at the hands of Set. Conqueror of all obstacles.

Ra - God of the Sun. Associated with healing and bringing abundance in life.

Bast - The Egyptian cat-headed Goddess. Associated with joy, happiness and pleasure.

Greek

Aphrodite - The Goddess of love, beauty and sexuality.

Apollo - The Greek God of the Sun. Associated with healing, the arts and inspiration.

Artemis - Goddess of the moon and nature. Protector of all life, especially women and children.

Hecate - Goddess of the underworld, magick, and the crossroads. Her night is the new moon, and she will aid in banishing negative energy.

Eros - God of love and sexual attraction.

Roman

Mercury - Messenger of the Gods. Associated with communication, thought and travel.

Jupiter - King of the Gods. Associated with mercy, compassion, wisdom, and luck.

Venus - Goddess of love, beauty, and sexuality.

Diana - Goddess of fertility. Also associated with the woods, hunting, and the moon.

Hindu

Krishna - Hindu God of love

Ganesha - God of intellect, communication, and remover of obstacles.

Lakshmi - Goddess of fortune and beauty. Bringer of good fortune, wealth and abundance.

Durga - India's mother Goddess. Associated with protection.

Kali - This is Durga's more aggressive form. In this form she is the destroyer of all evil. Her husband is Shiva, and he also is known as a destroyer of evil and God of transformation.

Celtic

Cernunnos - God of the hunt, Sun God. Associated with fertility, providing food.

Brigid - Goddess of healing, inspiration, crafts. Also associated with strength and perseverance.

Cerridwen - Goddess of the moon, the harvest. Associated with wisdom, inspiration, rebirth, and transformation.

Gwyddion - God of civilization. Associated with magick and positive transformation.

Norse

Odin - Father of the Gods, God of wisdom and prophesy. Is said to see all.

Thor - God of Thunder and the sky. Associated with strength, is a strong protector.

Freya - Goddess of love and fertility. Also associated with magick, astral travel.

Since, over the years, there have been many different Pagan religions and many Gods and Goddesses, I feel it's important to list examples here. I personally have felt the presence of several deities. Ganesha is joyful and full of wisdom. Isis is very strong, motherly and protective. Horus is ever vigilant and ready to right wrongs in society. The Wiccan creation story basically states that The All came first. The Lord and Lady were born from the All and all of creation came from their union. The many various Gods and Goddesses basically can be seen as various aspects of the Lord and Lady or part of the Divine order. Though there is only one base Divine source, there are many beings who could be considered part of this order, including Gods, Goddesses, Angels, Guides and Masters. A master is a Soul who has already mastered karmic lessons on Earth, like for example, the Buddha. In ancient Egypt the Priests were great teachers and after they died, they would have a temple set aside on the astral Plane where they would continue to teach after their death. Their students were given the keys to these Astral realms, which were locked, and they could reach them through astral travel. They had only to do the proper meditation to unlock the door. Anubis was the God commonly called upon to assist with astral travel, as well as helping the dead cross over to the next world. The Priest would stay and teach there for a while before finally moving on to rejoin with the All. A very structured and complex system. Not to worry though, everybody has at least one Spirit Guide. I will be covering your Guides and how to contact them in the Occult Aspects chapter. It's also said that everyone has at least one Guardian Angel. They are often there to give you invisible help when you really need it the most. That's not to say that people are invincible and can never be hurt, obviously. But sometimes when you're about to make a really big mistake and it's just not your time to go yet, they may step in and assist you.

I find it fascinating that these pantheons have so many similarities. Even in the lore, the story of the Greek Gods and their battle with the Titans is somewhat reminiscent of the story of the Hindu Gods and their great battle with Demons. The stories of the Hindu Goddess Kali-Ma and the Egyptian Goddess Sekhmet. Both were so intense with fury in their missions to destroy evil that they went completely out of control and had to be tricked into calming down once the evil was gone. The Greeks at one time considered the Egyptian Gods and Goddesses their own, only with different names. The simple fact that so many civilizations even shared the belief in multiple Gods ans Goddesses, with often similar tales, is fascinating. Some consider this an indication that all humanity shares a common experience. Some might even suggest that the more common stories and beliefs could date back events that took place on the lost continent of Atlantis. Some say it's likely that Stonehenge was built by descendants of Atlantis, who later became the Druids. The existence of this ancient civilization has yet to be proven, of course, but it is, nevertheless, believed by many people.

The great psychic Edgar Cayce mentioned Atlantis often in his readings, and even stated that the Atlantean records were hidden underground near the right paw of the Sphinx. He also said that one day these records would be uncovered, and when they were, it would shake up everything and knock humanity on its collective ear! I will leave it up to the reader to decide on Atlantis, but personally, I would LOVE to see that happen!

Chapter 8

Occult aspects

The Aura

This section will deal with the occult aspects of Wicca. For those who don't know,

the occult simply means "the unseen". For example, the astral plane is unseen by the human eye.

Yet it is possible to see it if your third eye is open. Clairvoyants can see the astral plane, and

even read auras. Your third eye is located between your eyebrows. It's said to be the remnant

a third astral "eye" possessed by our earliest ancestors. This enabled them to see what was going

on in astral plane, while their two physical eyes viewed the material world. Over time, as people

became more and more involved with their physical lives, this ability deteriorated. The exercises

in the meditation/visualization chapter will help to slowly awaken this ability.

One thing that can be seen astrally, but not with the physical eye, is the AURA. Your

aura is an energy field that surrounds your body. When seen, on a basic level, it contains a blend

of colors that can reveal much about your personality, your mood, and even your health. Your

aura can be strengthened and even expanded by techniques like the Tower of Light. Some things

that can weaken your aura include poor diet, lack of exercise, lack of fresh air, lack of rest,

alcohol, drugs, and improper psychic activity.

Chakras

Chakras are another part of you that are unseen. Basically, these are small, spinning

balls of energy that run along your spine. Each one is a different color and governs a different

function. Here is a list starting from the bottom and going up:

1. Root Chakra

Element: Earth

Color: Red

Governs: survival, security.

Located: At the base of your spine.

Sacral Chakra

Element: Water

Color: Orange

Governs: emotions , sexuality, creativity, and sense of taste

Located: Just below your belly button.

Solar Plexus Chakra

Element: Fire

Color: Yellow

Governs: energy, motivation

Located: Between solar plexus and naval

Heart Chakra

Element: Air

Color: Pink and Green

Located: chest

Governs: Your ability to love. This is where your basic Earthly needs connect to your higher spiritual needs.

Throat Chakra

Element: Ether

Color: Blue

Located: throat

Governs: Intuition

Third Eye Chakra

Element: Light/Telepathic energy

Color: Indigo

Governs: Higher Intuition

Located: Brow

Crown Chakra

Element: Thought

Color: Violet, gold, white

Governs: Wisdom and spiritual enlightenment.

Located: top of head

Note how the Chakras range from your most basic Earthly needs at the bottom to your higher spiritual needs at the top. The trick is to try and balance these Chakras.if one spins too fast, there will be too much activity in that area. Too slow, and there is not enough. For example, if your heart Chakra spins too slow, you will struggle with being able to give love.

There are stones that can aid you with balancing your Chakras. The simplest technique is to meditate on the element and color of the one your trying to balance. While you meditate, have the appropriate stone placed on or near the Chakra. Here are the stones most recommended:

Root: Smokey Quartz

Sacral: Carnelian

Solar Plexus: Argonite

Heart: Rose Quartz

Throat: Sodalite

Third Eye: Lapis Lazuli
Crown: Amethyst

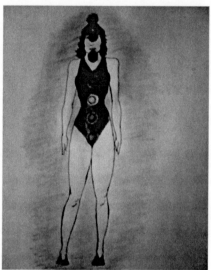

Chakra Locations

Astral Travel

Another thing worth mentioning here is astral travel. Astral travel, as the name

suggests, is when you actually leave your body and go traveling through the astral plane. It's perfectly safe and there's no chance of getting stuck or not being able to find your way back. You are attached to your body with a silver cord which will snap you back into your body if anything bad is happening at the house. The cord will never be broken as long as you're alive, and will go with you anywhere you go. Astral traveling is something you do all the time when you're asleep anyway. Learning how to do it consciously, however, may take a lot of practice. One of the simplest ways to practice this is to lie on your stomach and go into a meditative state. Then try to picture yourself with your back against the ceiling looking down at yourself. Eventually, you will find yourself actually doing it. This may come easily for some, and for others it may take a little more work. Of course, there's really no hurry, so relax. Everybody does things at their own pace.

Spirit Guide

One of the best and most important experiences you will have is when you meet your Spirit Guide. I have met mine. So has my wife, and so have many of our Wiccan friends. So how do you meet your Spirit Guide? The answer is simple : your Guide will appear to you when you're ready. How will you see your Guide? Your Guide may appear to you in a dream, or may appear sometime when you are meditating. Your Guide may appear as male or female or even as an animal. The form your Guide takes depends on you. Your Spirit Guide knows you and will only take on a form that you will trust. For example, if you have issues with trusting people, your Guide may take the form of an animal. If you have a hard time trusting men, your Guide may appear as a woman, etc. pay close attention when you see your Guide, as he/she will usually have a very important message for you. Sometimes you may ask a question of your Guide and he/she will have an answer for you. Remember that your Guide is no ordinary ghost, but a higher spiritual being. He/she will always point you in the right direction.

Energy Bodies

Your Guide is already a highly developed being, but you too are connected to the Divine. As stated previously, we are all much more than simply physical beings, we have our built in connections. You've already learned about your chakras and your astral body, but there's more. Human beings actually have roughly seven energy bodies, as noted by clairvoyants. Exactly how many is up for some debate, as they blend together and create different layers, so they may appear differently to different people. The classic diagram, first drawn up by the ancient Egyptians, shows seven. Others list 5 or 8. Here, I will list the basic 5 to give an idea of what exactly they consist of. Much like your chakras, you begin with the Earth bound and go out to the highest plane which is the Spiritual.

Physical body - This body you are already familiar with. It's purely physical and allows you to function here on the physical plane. Your energy bodies each have a different appearance and extend out just a little further from this one.

Etheric body - This body is made up of higher and finer vibrations than your physical form' therefore making it invisible to the naked eye. Much the same way you cant see ultraviolet light. It's a bridge between you and the ether, and it's said that it enables you absorb positive and beneficial energies that your body needs. It's an exact duplicate of your physical body with all parts included.

Emotional body - This is a body that appears as swirling colors. These colors represent your emotional state. The brighter colors represent happiness and the muddier ones represent confused emotions.

Mental body - Here we enter the realm of thought. Your thoughts actually come to life on the mental plane. The ones you put the most energy into thinking can actually seek to manifest on the physical plane and the ones you think the most can influence your life as well. So the

lesson here is be careful what you think !

Etheric Template body - This body exists in the Spiritual Plane and it's actually the template

for all your other bodies (meaning it came first). It is your connection to Divine will. When your

will is in tune with Divine will, powerful and beneficial changes occur and your life is

transformed.

Numerology

Numerology is a tool that many Wiccans utilize to determine their path in life. It's also a

tool used when choosing a magickal name. The first thing we do is calculate our Life Path

Number and Destiny Number. Your Life Path Number shows you what path you will be taking

in life and your Destiny Number shows what your ultimate goal in this life will be. Here's the

Numerology chart:

your numbers, you only
formula. Here's an
example, using the
Joe Smith. First, match

corresponding number
the destiny number

Now, to calculate
have to follow the

fictitious name John
the letters with the

from the chart: I'll do
first.

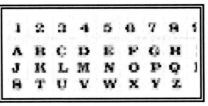

John Joe Smith

1685 165 14928

Now add the numbers of the first name and reduce: 1+6+8+5 = 20. Reduce: 2+0 = 2.

Middle name: 1+6+5 = 12. Reduce = 1+2 = 3.

Last name: 1+4+9+2+8 = 24. 2+4 = 6.

Now we have to add the totals to get the Destiny Number. 2+3+6 = 11. 1+1 = 2

So John's Destiny Number would be 2. Your Destiny Number tells you what your highest goal will be in this lifetime. Your Lifepath Number gives you an idea of what tools you have to work with to achieve that goal. To calculate your Lifepath Number, all you need is your birth date. Let's say your date of birth is 6/8/1978. You would have to add up the numbers of the year. 1+9+7+8 = 25. 2+5 = 7. Now add that with the Month and day: 6+8+7 = 21. 2+1 = 3. So your Lifepath Number would be 3.

Chapter 9

The Sabbats

Here, we will briefly cover and describe the Wiccan holidays. As Wicca is a nature based religion, so too do the holidays coincide with events that take place in nature. These days are called the Sabbats, and they make up The Wheel of the Year. The story of the Lord and Lady is also told during the year, as The Lord is born, grows to full strength, and dies, only to be reborn again in the Lady's womb. Every year this cycle is repeated, and it begins with the Witches' New Year which is known as Samhain (usually pronounced SOW- en). We celebrate these holidays mainly because it helps us to be in tune with nature, which is something that every Witch needs.

Samhain Oct. 31

This is my favorite of all the holidays, and a favorite of many Wiccans that I know. Although it's the part of the year where the Lord dies, and the Lady begins to go into mourning, it's also the time when we honor our own departed relatives and ancestors. Some people do this by simply preparing a meal and setting a place for the one (or ones) they choose to honor. Often the favorite meal of a departed relative will be prepared and set out symbolically for that person. It's also known as the time of the year when the veil between the worlds is the thinnest and it's a great time for meditating and scrying.

Yule Dec 21

This is also known as the Winter Solstice. It's the return of light, as the days begin to grow longer again. It's also the time when the Lord is reborn again from the Lady's womb. These are represented by the lighting of the Yule log. Traditionally, the log is either Pine or Oak, as these woods are associated with the Lord. Decorating a tree and hanging mistletoe are also fun. Mistletoe is actually a protective herb for the home.

Imbolc Feb 2

On this day, after a long Winter, we begin to look towards Spring. We know that soon life will be springing up again, and the Earth will once again become fertile. We celebrate and prepare for this by getting rid of things that we have outgrown, and making way for the new. The Lady recovers from giving birth, and the Lord is seen as a young child.

Ostara Mar 21

Ostara is the Spring Equinox. Easter is a Christianized version of this holiday, and eggs and rabbits have been symbols of fertility since the times of ancient Egypt. At this time of year we may bless seeds in preparation for planting. Both figuratively and literally. The Lord is growing to maturity now. As the Earth is waking up, the Lady is making everything fertile again, as she herself is becoming fertile.

Beltane Apr 30

On this day, the Lord has reached manhood, and his union with the Lady is celebrated. This union is said to bring the renewal of life and growth, as things begin to turn green and grow once again. Dancing around the Maypole is a way to celebrate the Lord, while the cauldron is celebrated as a symbol of the Lady, who is said to be impregnated by the Lord at this time.

Summer Solstice Jun 21

On this, the longest day of the year, the Sun is at it's peak, and so are the powers of the Lord and the Lady. Once celebrated by jumping over bonfires, this practice has faded in modern times due to laws regarding fire hazards. Still, we give reverence, and it is an excellent day for magick. Spells can be done at this time to promote fertility, love and renewal.

Lughnassad Aug 2

This is the beginning of the fall harvest. We celebrate this by having a feast. Traditionally bread is also baked on this day, and the altar is decorated with fruits and vegetables. It's a celebration of nature's abundance. At this time, the Lord's strength is waning as the days grow shorter. But even as he wanes, he is being reborn in the womb of the Lady.

Mabon Sep 21

This is the Autumnal equinox. Day and night are of equal length again, and winter is near. It's also the last celebration of the Fall harvest. We celebrate this day by decorating the altar with a cornucopia. A last celebration of nature's bounty before the coming winter. The Lord grows ever weaker and the Lady prepares for his death at Samhain.

The story of the God that dies and is reborn may sound vaguely familiar. To me, it's reminiscent of the story of Osiris, Isis and Horus. In this story Osiris is killed by his brother Set, and his body parts are scattered across Egypt. Isis gathers his parts and uses magick to take in his essence and create Horus. Horus goes on to unite Egypt and Osiris lives on as the Lord of the afterlife. The ancient Egyptians also celebrated seasonal holidays, as have many other Pagan cultures.

The Wiccan holidays are known as the greater and lesser Sabbats. The lesser Sabbats are marked by the changing of the seasons, while the greater ones are midway points. The midway point is when the particular season is at it's peak, so these are days of power. The best time for invoking the male energy, obviously, is midsummer. The two Equinoxes also mark the points when day and night are of equal length.

Esbats

Esbats are celebrations held in honor of the Goddess. They are usually held under full Moon, though they can be held during any phase of the Moon. It's said that the Lord chose the Sun as his symbol and the Lady chose the Moon. They are reminders for those of us here on Earth. The Esbats are supposed to be held once a month. They are usually done outside, and you can do them alone, or with a group of Wiccan friends or family. Items you may need for ritual include : your altar, silver, quartz crystals, and a cauldron or fire proof bowl. Say your prayers for the Goddess and then enjoy white wine and crescent cakes. The full moon is an especially good time to charge ritual tools, and, of course, it's a powerful time to do magick with Lunar energy. And remember when the moon is waxing (getting bigger) is the best time to start new projects. When the Moon is waning (Getting smaller) is the best time to banish things (like negative energy, bad habits, or other things that are causing you harm). If you need to draw on the Goddess energy, you can also draw down the Moon. To do this, simply stand under the full Moon with feet apart and arms extended. Your hands should be slightly above your shoulders. Visualize a white streaming light coming down from the Moon and filling your body. You can also draw down the Sun this way, but you stand with your arms folded, hands resting on your shoulders.

Chapter 10

The Underlying Theme

This section deals with comparative religions. Some people are just bombarded since birth with a certain belief system. They subscribe to only one religion, because it's the only one they know. It's good to keep an open mind. You can learn a lot from other religions. The teachings of Buddha and Jesus are great examples. One thing I've found studying the world's major religions is that there is an underlying similarity between many of them. Yes, we've all heard it before. The raging conservative Christian that blasts you and tells you you're condemned to Hell if you keep practicing Witchcraft. But how can they say that when the Bible tells them not to judge, differentiate, or discriminate against other people and to love thy neighbor? And how can they say this when only a percentage of the population believes this? Let's take a look at religions of the world, and instead of focusing on the differences, we'll look at some of the similarities between Wicca and other religions.

Hindus believe in karma and reincarnation. They also have a whole pantheon of Gods and Goddesses, so the male and female aspect of the Divine is also represented there. Hindus also are very aware of the astral plane. Some even sharing meals with their God, that the God is believed to consume the astral (spiritual) portion of. Very similar to the offerings some Witches make. They also have some very unique and effective meditation techniques, as well as Yoga positions to help balance your chakras.

Buddhists also are heavily into meditation. They believe in the philosophy of not causing any harm. They believe in karma and reincarnation and work towards achieving enlightenment and freeing themselves from the karmic cycle to rejoin with the Divine. It's a very peaceful religion that never preaches against other religions, or seeks to convert others.

Shamans practice spiritual healing techniques, herbal medicine, meditation and various methods of inducing visions. They have methods of astral travel, and contacting the higher spiritual realms as well. One of the more fascinating practices is that of soul recovery. Traumatic events of the past are said to cause tiny fragments of your aura or soul self to break off. The Shaman can actually travel the astral plane to recover these and re-integrate them.

Catholicism is actually a combination of Christianity and Paganism. It was created in ancient Rome by Emperor Constantine at a time when his empire was divided and he wanted desperately to keep it together. The roman Gods basically were replaced by Saints and some of their rituals still seem very Pagan.

Christianity seems to have nothing in common at all with Wicca, but actually it does. The teachings of Jesus are actually very much like the Wiccan Rede. He was a peaceful man that did not engage in violence and asked his to love their fellow man. Many have also noticed the similarity between his story and the stories of older Pagan deities. A direct correlation has been drawn between the stories of Jesus and Horus specifically. It's true that Isis giving birth to Horus was the original immaculate conception. The name Satan even seems to derived from Set-An, the name Set was commonly known by in ancient Egypt. The exchange between Jesus and Satan is reminiscent of the exchange between Siddhartha (Buddha) and Mara the king of Demons. The creation story was taken from Mesopotamia. Some people believe that the stories in the Bible are just total ripoffs other cultures and that there was, in fact, never any Jesus. Others suggest that it's the same soul that keeps reincarnating to teach. I believe there have been many great spiritual teachers. Some of which may have indeed been the same soul coming back.

They all serve a Divine purpose. They all teach similar ethics. Most have taught about karma and reincarnation. Yes, Christianity originally taught that too.

Of course there is an underlying anti-Christian attitude among some Pagans as well. This is mainly due to the fact that a lot of Christians use angry, hateful and condemning words towards them. It's also partly due to the fact that in ancient times they used to burn and hang people suspected of being Witches . Hate begets hate and violence begets violence. Is this the message that Jesus, a peaceful man by all accounts, meant to spread? I don't think so. The original teachings of Christianity were lost along the way. Mainly due to the selfish interests of a few who wanted to have power over many. Even today, televangelists still sit in front of a television camera and insist that God said people have to send them money.

Some Wiccans used to be Christians and simply left because they were disgusted with acts like these. In a way you could say that Wiccans follow the teachings of Jesus better than some Christians. But the real point is that more and more people are waking up and realizing that we are all human. We are all in the same boat. There is no need to feel completely separate from the Divine, when it's a part of all of us. There is no need for women to be made to feel inferior. There is no need to condemn someone to "Hell" just because they were born gay or lesbian, or because they were born Hindu or Muslim.

And what is "Hell" anyway? Wiccans have no belief in a place where a soul goes to burn in flames, or suffer for all eternity. Does it make sense that the Divine would create souls only to discard them in such a manner? That would be a waste of time and material. Hell is more a place of your own making when you think about it. You can make it Hell for yourself by your own negative actions.

It's time for people to wake up and realize that we're all human and we're all in the same boat here. With the astrological age of Aquarius upon us, changes are said to be taking place. Astrologers will tell you that this will be a great Spiritual awakening and the world will be united in brotherhood. While it's hard for me to say just exactly how this will come about, or to what extent, I am very optimistic about this. You can already see changes happening. Look around and you will see Wiccan and Neo Pagan movement growing. People don't want to be spoon-fed someone else's ideas, they want to experience the Divine connection for themselves. They don't want to feel separated from the Divine, but closer to it. The discovery of Quantum Physics is another clear sign, as it gives scientists an opportunity to study the true fabric of the universe. They have already learned there is much more going on than originally suspected. A direct link has even been established between Quantum Physics and Vedic metaphysics. Keep in mind that Astrology is much more than just your daily Horoscope. It's an occult science and it takes years of study to really master. The energies of the planets really have been shown to have a direct influence on Earthly life. But whether you choose to believe the stars or not, the changes are still occurring rapidly. The Mayans were masters of Astrology, and though their religious beliefs also were altered at some point to include horrible acts of human sacrifice, their charts and maps of the stars, and how they would look 1000s of years after the charts were made, were dead on accurate. Quite impressive for people who weren't known for having ANYTHING like the technology we have now. Their illustrations depicting the events of 2012 (which apparently marks the end of a cycle) show large beings, perhaps Gods and Goddesses, pouring water over the Earth.

There is a lot of speculation, and some fear, about what that is supposed to mean. One very obvious literal translation of that would be massive rain and floods. Some may say it represents the ocean rising and causing floods due to global warming. While it's quite possible that may happen to some extent, I think it's important to keep in mind that they were Astrologers. Water is also very symbolic of the Aquarian age coming on, much the same way that the fish was symbolic of Pisces. Since Aquarius promises an ultimately positive outcome, my stance is to stay away from the coastlines, and hope for the best.

Chapter 11

Herbal Remedies

Here I've decided to include some simple herbal remedies for everyday illnesses. We get requests for these on the groups from time to time, and they come in handy. There are many types of Wiccans. Some choose to be vegetarian or vegan, and some choose to consume only organic foods. Some will choose only herbal remedies and refuse to pollute their body with chemicals. Some will simply take acetaminophen when they have a headache. Whichever type of Wiccan you choose to be, I'm sure you will find this information useful. Just be sure to check with your physician before using any unfamiliar herbs, as some could cause an allergic reaction, or interact with medications you already are on. These remedies are generally safe, but use at your own risk.

1. Allergies - Garlic is used for it's anti-inflammatory effects. Nettles may be taken as a tincture for hay fever symptoms.

2. Anxiety - This can be soothed with Chamomile tea. A tincture of flower essences is recommended for sudden stressful situations. Chamomile and Lavender are very good for relaxation. Try Wild Rose Flower for improving family interactions during times of disharmony.

3. Colds and flu - Echinacea and Boneset tinctures are known to stimulate the immune system. For coughs try Mullein and Boneset. Use an Elder flower tincture to treat fevers for children.

4. Constipation - Cascara Sagrada, Dandelion Root, Yellow Dock Root, or Aloe Vera juice are all good remedies for this. A Thyme steam bath is great for relieving coughs and congestion. Also good is Onion Soup. It can help reduce fever, infection, swelling, and sore throat.

5. Depression and sadness - Rub Neroli essential oil on the soles of your feet. Citrus essential oils mixed with water in a spray bottles are also very uplifting when sprayed in the air. For long term or frequently occurring bouts of sadness, take St. John's Wort in capsules or tincture.

6. Headache - If you have a headache and fell overheated, try a cooling Lavender Tea or a

Lavender tincture. You can also rub Lavender essential oil on your forehead. For a headache with chills, try Rosemary tea, or tincture, or rub Rosemary essential oil on your forehead. Be careful not to use undiluted essential oils, as they may cause welts and blistering. Feverfew is used to help prevent migraines. It can be made into a tea, or taken in capsule form (85 milligrams per capsule).

7. Upset stomach - Peppermint is always good for indigestion. (Unless you are pregnant, in which case you should avoid peppermint)Ginger capsules are good for nausea. Ginger essential oil, massaged into the soles of your feet will often stop vomiting right away. Slippery Elm bark provides relief for upset stomach, as well as cough and sore throat.

8. Injuries - You can treat sprains, sore muscles or joints by applying Arnica oil directly to the injury. St. Johns Wort oil has anti-inflammatory affects. It's good for treating nerve pain and Sciatica.

9. Insomnia - Take California Poppy, Chamomile, or Passionflower before going to bed to help induce sleep. Also, Lavender essential oil rubbed into the temples, or sprayed around your bed or on your pillow, can help promote relaxation, restful sleep and pleasant dreams.

10. Skin conditions - Try Calendula tincture, oil, or gel for cuts, sores, insect bites, stings, sunburns and rashes. Apple Cider Vinegar is a strong anti-fungal and disinfectant. A Chamomile steam bath can clear up acne and oily skin. A Garlic paste can reduce swelling and pain if rubbed on an injured area. It also cleans the blood, and helps fight infection. Comfrey is known to aid in new cell growth and help heal wounds. Cover scrapes or clean cuts with a bruised leaf to speed up healing. Do not ingest Comfrey, it's for outside use only.

11. Infections - Goldenseal is known for it's antibiotic properties. You can make a with the powdered root. Add ½ to 1 teaspoon to 1 cup of water. Let it steep up to 10 minutes. The

recommended dose is 3 cups a day. Cranberry juice is a natural remedy for bladder infections, and contains a natural antibiotic as well.

Making A Tincture

To make a tincture, you will need a clean glass jar with a tight fitting lid, some good alcohol preferably clear 190 proof, and, of course, your herbs! Use as much of the herb as you think you will need for the tincture, you will need to grind the herb into a fine powder. Use just enough alcohol to cover the herb. You may also charge the herb with a magickal intention. Put the lid on tight and shake the mixture up. Store in a dark place, like a cabinet, for 7-10 days. When the alcohol takes on the color of the herb, then strain it through cheesecloth into a clean glass jar with a tight fitting lid. Your tincture is ready to use.

These are all natural remedies that Witches have known about for generations, and even though the FDA refuses to test them, they work.

Herbs in Magick

Of course, herbs are also used in magick. Often they are burned as incense in the circle. Some Witches see this as a way of carrying their message up to the Gods. Usually, you can find ready made incenses for all your needs at a metaphysical store. Some Witches prefer to make their own. Grinding your own herbs with a mortar and pestle gives you a great chance to put your own energy into the herbs. Other ways to use herbs include making healing poppets, which can be used to help a sick friend (a poppet is a doll made of cloth, usually filled with empowered healing herbs), dream pillows, which can help promote prophetic or pleasant dreams, or simply carrying a pouch filled with empowered herbs for a particular magickal purpose. Here, I will list some of the popular herbs and botanicals used in Witchcraft, along with their purpose in magick.

Angelica- Protection/hex breaking, healing, visions.

Burdock- Healing, protection.

Carnation- Strength & vitality, healing, protection.

Dandelion- Good fortune, divination.

Dill- Protection, money, love or lust.

Dragon's Blood- Protection, power enhancement.

Elderberries- Protection, prosperity, banishing negativity.

Frankincense- Banishing, consecrating, protection, spirituality.

Gardenia- Healing, love, spirituality.

Ginseng- Vitality, healing, love or lust.

Horehound- Banishing, protection, healing, enhance mental abilities.

Jasmine- Love, money, dreams.

Juniper- Love, health, protection, banishing.

Lavender- Relaxation, sleep, meditation.

Mugwort- Clairvoyance, divination, dreams, astral projection, strength, protection.

Orris- Love, divination, protection.

Passion flower- Sleep, peace, friendship.

Pine- Protection, fertility, money, banish negative entities.

Poppy- Love, money, luck.

Rose- Love, beauty, psychic powers.

Rue- Curse-breaking, healing, mental powers.

Sage- Purification, wisdom, prosperity, relaxation.

Slippery Elm- Stop gossip and slander.

Star Anise- Psychic abilities, luck.

Valerian- Sleep, love, purification.

Vetivert- Love, money, luck.

Violet- Love, lust, healing, peace, protection.

Willow- Divination, healing, protection, love.

Witch Hazel- Protection, emotional healing.

Wormwood- Love, protection, psychic abilities, safe travel.

Glossary

Astral Plane - The realm beyond the physical. Unseen by human eyes, because it consists of higher energy vibrations. In this realm, time and space are meaningless.

Aura - Your personal energy field. All living things have an aura, which exists on the astral plane, and consists of several layers.

Buddha - Main figure in the religion of Buddhism. A man named Siddhartha, who sat in meditation until he achieved enlightenment.

Chakras - Chakra comes from the Sanskrit word "cakra" meaning "wheel". The chakras are spinning energy centers in the body that run along the spine.

Higher Self - Your highest spiritual self, the part of you that is closest to the Divine.

Lady - Another name for the Goddess, female manifestation of the Divine.

Lord - Another name for the God, male manifestation of the Divine.

Magick - The use of natural psychic energies, with intent, to create change. Spelled with a "k" to differentiate from stage magic.

Neo-Pagan - A person who practices a modern version of one of the various pre-Christian religions.

Sabbats - Natural holidays celebrated by Pagans.

Spirit Guide - Higher, enlightened spirit who is there to offer you guidance.

Wicca - A Neo-Pagan religion. Recognized as a legal religion in the United States.

Witch - One who practices Witchcraft.

Witchcraft - Similar to magick, a ritual where magick is performed.

Suggested Reading

Alder, Vera Stanley- The Finding of the Third Eye. 1970 Samuel Weiser

Buckland, Raymond- Practical Candleburning Rituals. 2006 Llewellyn

Campbell, Dan- Edgar Cayce on the Power of Color, Stones, and Crystals. 1989 Warner Bros

Cunningham, Scott- Cunningham's Encyclopedia of Magickal Herbs. Expanded and Revised Edition 2005, Llewellyn

Cunningham, Scott- Wicca, A Guide for the Solitary Practitioner. 1988 Llewellyn

De Angeles, Ly- Witchcraft, Theory and Practice. 2000 Llewellyn

Denning, Melita and Phillips, Osbourne- The Llewellyn Practical Guide to Psychic Self Defense and Well Being. 1995 Llewellyn

Goldberg, Dr. Bruce- Protected by the Light. 1998 Llewellyn

Hewitt, William- Psychic Development for Beginners. 2003 Llewellyn

Zimmerman, Denise and Gleason, Catherine- The Complete Idiots Guide to Wicca and Withcraft. 2000 Alpha Books

Zolar, Zolar's Encyclopedia of Ancient and Forbidden Knowledge. 1984 Arco

Lightning Source UK Ltd.
Milton Keynes UK
24 November 2009

146659UK00002B/228/P